D1102476

This book has been published by Marlow Foods Limited, Premier House, Centrium Business Park, Griffiths Way, St. Albans. AL1 2RE, United Kingdom

www.quorn.co.uk

First published by Marlow Foods Limited 2010

© 2010 Marlow Foods Limited

Designed by INITIALS Marketing Limited

Food photography © Gus Filgate
Life style photography © Jamie Maxwell Photography

ISBN Number: 978-0-9566088-0-2

Printed and bound in Great Britain by Matthews The Printers Limited

All rights reserved. No part of this publication may be reproduced, stored in a retrieval system, or transmitted in any form, or by any means, electronic, mechanical, photocopying, recording, or otherwise, without the prior written permission of the publishers.

Mixed Sources
Product group from well-managed forests and other controlled sources
www.fsc.org Cert no. BV-COC-958988
© 1996 Forest Stewardship Council
FSC

Find out more about the Quorn brand and Quorn products at www.quorn.co.uk

QUORN and the QUORN Logo are registered trademarks of Marlow Foods Limited

We would like to thank the following members of the team for working so hard towards ensuring the success of The Quorn Kitchen;

Kate, Carole, Margaret, Anna, Ita, everyone in the development team in Stokesley, Gus, Nicole, Elaine, Penny, Rafi, Lucy, Aman, Kathryn, Adam, Karen, Kim, Rosinda, Claire, Jo, Sophie, JoAnna, Helen, Chris, Simon, Greg, Toby, Phil, Ernie and everyone else who has helped.

Welcome...

... to The Quorn® Kitchen Recipe Book.

By popular demand, we felt it only right to don our aprons, get imaginative and bring the taste of our kitchen to yours.

More and more of us are becoming confident in the kitchen and creative with home cooking. There's an abundance of cooking shows on the television to inspire us, countless recipe books by famous chefs and a huge variety of ingredients on offer. Here at Quorn HQ, we think this is great, but none of them seem to talk about Quorn products as delicious ingredients for the every day cook, and how to cook them well.

The breadth of Quorn products, accompanied by their versatility and championed by their great taste as well as your continual requests, is to us, more than enough reason to bring out the 'Quorn Kitchen Recipe Book'. With a pinch of imagination and a twist of inspiration, we have rustled up a collection of recipes to suit all tastes, and every occasion.

We hope you enjoy creating and eating the dishes just as much as we enjoyed putting this book together. So break out of your old habits, get those pages turning, and cook up some great tasting Quorn dishes.

Contents

Recipes
for success

Quorn® products are just for vegetarians, right? Well, actually these days some of our biggest fans don't think of themselves as vegetarian at all. They simply want to go easy on the meat and follow a healthier, lighter, more balanced diet.

Interestingly, the roots of the Quorn brand are more humanitarian than vegetarian. It all started in the mid 1960s. Our founder, Lord Rank, saw serious global protein shortages looming.

So he set out to develop a nutritious protein that could feed the world, and after many years of development, the Quorn brand of meat-free foods was born.

So what's behind the Quorn brand? Well, at the heart of all Quorn products is a healthy protein ingredient called mycoprotein, a nutritious member of the fungi family, like mushrooms and truffles.

This fantastic source of protein is used to make our products, most of which are lower in fat, saturates and calories than meat, PLUS it's cholesterol free and has no trans fats at all.

But more important than any of that, Quorn dishes taste great. Quorn products can be used to make all of your everyday favourites – stews, casseroles, stir-fries and pasta dishes – and so much more besides.

Enjoy.

Simple
Sharing
Snacks

A selection of
easy-to-make delicious
recipes, perfect for
sharing, that are sure
to go down a treat.

Salsa & Nacho Crusted Fillets

Preparation Time: 5 mins
Cooking Time: 14 mins
Serves: 2-3

1 pack Quorn Chicken Style Fillets
200g tub fresh tomato salsa
40g Nachos, crushed
25g Monterey Jack cheese or
Cheddar cheese, grated (optional)

1. Pre-heat oven to 200°C (400°F/Gas Mark 6) and lightly oil a baking tray.

2. Place the fillets on the baking tray and spoon equal amounts of salsa on top of each one. Bake for 7 minutes.

3. Remove from oven and sprinkle the crushed Nachos over the top of each fillet and top with the grated cheese.

4. Bake on the middle shelf of the oven for a further 7 minutes, until the cheese is golden and bubbling.

Butternut Squash Tart

We would like to thank Claire Chilvers for submitting this recipe to us — a great addition we hope you'll agree!

Preparation Time: 10 mins
Cooking Time: 30 mins
Serves: 4

175g of Quorn Chicken Style Pieces

1 sheet of ready rolled short-crust pastry

1 tbsp olive oil

125g butternut squash peeled and cut into small cubes (1cm cube approx.)

1 onion, finely diced

2 tsp dried rosemary

125g pack Welsh goats cheese (soft cheese in a log)

2-3 tbsp milk or water

1. Pre-heat the oven to 200°C (400°F/Gas Mark 6). Line a lightly greased flan tin (20cm in diameter) with the pastry and allow to rest.

2. Meanwhile fry the butternut squash and onion for 2 minutes in the olive oil, then add the Quorn Pieces and continue to fry for 5 minutes or until golden brown, stirring occasionally.

3. Remove from the heat and add the rosemary and goats cheese, mix well and let the cheese melt, add 2-3 tbsp of water or milk until the sauce is the consistency of double cream, season to taste.

4. Pour the mixture into the prepared pastry case and cook in the oven for 20 minutes.

Serve with new potatoes and crispy green salad leaves.

Blue Cheese Filled
Mushrooms

A great light lunch that's easy to throw together and tastes just as moreish as it looks.

Preparation Time: 5 mins
Cooking Time: 20 mins
Serves: 4

300g Quorn Steak Style Strips or Quorn Pieces

1 tbsp oil

4 large flat mushrooms, stalks trimmed

100g blue cheese - Roquefort, Stilton, Dolcelatte all work well

20g fresh breadcrumbs

Rocket leaves to garnish

1. Pre-heat the oven to 180°C (350°F/ Gas Mark 4).

2. Heat 1tbsp of oil in a pan and cook the strips or pieces over a medium heat for 10 minutes.

3. Place the mushrooms on a baking tray and divide the strips or pieces between each of them.

4. Crumble the cheese on the top of the strips or pieces.

5. Finish off by sprinkling with the breadcrumbs and cook in the oven for 7-8 minutes.

6. Season with ground black pepper and serve on a bed of rocket leaves.

Beef
Empanadas

Preparation Time: 15 mins + 30 mins chilling
Cooking Time: 30 mins
Makes: 8

1 pack 175g of Quorn Seasoned Steak Strips or half a bag of Quorn Steak Style Strips

Pastry:
450g plain flour
2 tsp baking powder
½ tsp salt
60g butter, diced
60g vegetable fat, diced
200ml chilled water

Filling:
1 tbsp olive oil
½ onion
½ green pepper, finely diced
½ vegetable stock cube
2 cloves garlic, finely chopped
1 tsp paprika
½ tsp chilli powder
3 tbsp red wine
50g Emmental cheese, finely grated
1 free-range egg, beaten

1. Pre-heat the oven to 180°C (350°F/Gas Mark 4).

2. For the pastry, mix the flour, baking powder and salt together in a mixing bowl. Rub in the butter and fat until the mixture resembles fine breadcrumbs. Mix in just enough water to form a soft dough. Wrap in cling film and chill in the fridge for 30 minutes.

3. For the empanada filling, heat 1 tbsp of oil in a large frying pan. Fry the onion and pepper until soft. Add the Quorn Steak Style Strips, crumbled stock cube and garlic. Fry for 2 minutes. Stir in the spices and cook for 30 seconds. Add the red wine and stir until most of the liquid has evaporated. Season to taste. Remove from the heat, cover and allow to cool.

4. To make the empanadas, roll out the pastry onto a lightly floured surface to a thin sheet. Cut out 8 discs of pastry, approximately 15cm (6in) diameter.

5. Put 1 tbsp of the filling on each pastry disc and top with a little grated cheese. Brush the edges with a little egg and fold over to make a pasty shape. Seal the edges well together. Prick a steam hole in the top of each empanada. Glaze with the beaten egg and place on a greased and lined baking tray.

6. Bake for 20 minutes until the pastry is golden brown.

Serve hot or cold as a snack.

Steak Style Wrap

Preparation Time: 10 mins
Cooking Time: 10 mins
Makes: 6 wraps

150g Quorn Steak Strips or Quorn Pieces
1 tbsp vegetable oil
75g mushrooms, sliced
6 soft flour tortilla wraps
6 tbsp onion relish
Large handful rocket leaves
75g prepared roasted
peppers, sliced
25g sun blushed tomato, diced
10g black olives, quartered (optional)

1. Heat a frying pan over a medium heat and pre-heat the oil, cook the steak strips for 4 minutes, stir in the mushrooms and continue to cook for a further 4 minutes.

2. Place tortillas on a chopping board and spread with 1 tbsp of the onion relish per wrap then layer with the rocket.

3. Mix together the mushrooms and steak strips with the peppers, sun blushed tomatoes and olives, divide mixture between the tortillas and roll. If not eating immediately individually cling film each wrap and refrigerate.

Italian Style Ciabatta

This is a great recipe for a tasty light lunch or cut into fingers served as part of a buffet, it tastes delicious served hot or cold.

Preparation Time: 10 mins
Cooking Time: 12 mins
Serves: 4 for lunch or 12 cut into small fingers for buffet/party food

1 pack Quorn Sausages of your choice

1 tbsp vegetable oil

1 large ciabatta, halved lengthways

230g tin Italian style bruschetta topping, (chopped tomatoes, herbs and garlic)

25g pitted black olives, halved

4 tbsp fresh basil leaves, torn, plus extra for garnish

75g Mozzarella cheese, grated

25g Cheddar cheese, grated

1. Pre-heat the oven to 200°C (400°F/ Gas Mark 6). Cook the Quorn Sausages following back of pack instructions in the vegetable oil until golden brown, cut into thin slices.

2. Spread each side of the ciabatta with the bruschetta topping and then top with the Quorn Sausage, olives, torn basil leaves, Mozzarella cheese and Cheddar cheese. Season well with freshly ground black pepper.

3. Cook for 10-12 minutes or until the ciabatta is golden and the cheese is melted.

Garnish with basil leaves and serve immediately.

Sticky Sausage Skewers

If you want to do something a bit different with your Quorn Sausages, why not try this delicious recipe – it's great in the oven, or on the BBQ. Great as a party nibble, cut the sausages into four and skewer each piece with a cocktail stick.

Preparation Time: 5 mins
Cooking Time: 20 mins
Serves: 2-3 or more on a buffet table

1 pack Quorn Sausages, defrosted* if using frozen

4 tbsp mango chutney

1 tbsp olive oil

1 tbsp lemon juice

1 rounded tsp wholegrain mustard

1 red or yellow pepper, cut into large pieces

1 red onion, cut into thick slices

6 cherry tomatoes

6 button mushrooms

Skewers or kebab sticks - soak wooden skewers in water for 15 minutes before using if grilling or barbecuing

1. Pre-heat the oven to 190°C (375°F/Gas Mark 5) or grill. Mix the mango chutney, olive oil, lemon juice and mustard together in a bowl.

2. Cut the sausages into bite-sized pieces and coat with the mustard mix.

3. Thread the vegetable pieces onto the skewers or kebab sticks alternating with the sausage pieces.

4. Brush with any remaining glaze, place on an oven tray and bake in the oven for 17 minutes, or under a medium hot grill for 8-9 minutes, turning frequently. Also great on the barbecue.

* for defrost instructions refer to page 166

Leek & Thyme Pâté

A fantastic pâté that can be served on crusty bread or crackers, would make a great starter or lunch-time snack.

Preparation Time: 5 mins
Cooking Time: 12 mins + 1 hour chilling
Serves: 4-6

175g Quorn Pieces, defrosted* if using frozen

25g butter

1 medium leek washed and finely chopped

1 tsp fresh thyme leaves & extra sprigs for garnish

1 clove garlic, crushed

100ml white wine

150g low fat cream cheese

1. In a frying pan melt the butter over a medium heat, add the leeks and the thyme leaves, cook gently until the leeks are softened but not browned, approximately 5 minutes. Remove ¾ of the leeks and set aside.

2. Add the garlic, Quorn Pieces and wine to the pan, season and simmer until all the wine has been absorbed.

3. Remove from the heat and allow to cool a little. Blend the Quorn Pieces and leeks that have been cooked in the wine in a food processor until smooth.

4. Remove from food processor and add the cream cheese and the remaining leeks and mix well. Season to taste.

5. Transfer to a suitable serving dish, smooth the top and decorate with a sprig of thyme, cover and chill for at least 1 hour.

6. Keep refrigerated and consume within 3 days.

* for defrost instructions refer to page 166

Scrumptious
Light Bites

Need more than a nibble and less than a meal? This selection of light bites is sure to meet you in the middle.

Thai Salad

Preparation Time: 15 mins + 30 mins marinating
Cooking Time: 5 mins
Serves: 4

350g pack Quorn Pieces

1-2 tbsp Green Thai paste - you can use more or less paste depending on how hot and spicy you like it

2 tbsp vegetable oil

125g green beans, cut into bite-sized pieces

175g white cabbage, finely shredded

2 medium sized tomatoes, de-seeded and diced

1 small red pepper, de-seeded and thinly sliced

1 medium mango, peeled and diced into 1cm cubes

1 tbsp fresh coriander, chopped

For the dressing:

Grated zest and juice of 1 lime

1 garlic clove, crushed

1cm piece fresh root ginger, peeled and finely grated

2 tsp soy sauce

4 tsp olive oil

Salad leaves and coriander leaves to serve

1. Marinate the Quorn Pieces in the Thai paste for 30 minutes.

2. Heat the oil in a small frying pan. Add the Quorn Pieces and cook for 5 minutes over a medium to high heat stirring constantly until golden in colour and set aside.

3. Blanch the green beans in boiling water for 1 minute, then refresh in cold water. Place in a bowl with the cabbage, tomatoes, pepper and mango. Stir in the Quorn Pieces and coriander, then season. Cover and chill in a refrigerator.

4. Mix together the dressing ingredients. Just before serving, drizzle the dressing over the salad and toss well. Serve on a bed of mixed salad leaves and garnish with coriander.

Fresh crusty bread is the ideal accompaniment.

Sausage, Roasted Pepper & Rocket Salad

Preparation Time: 5 mins
Cooking Time: 15 mins
Serves: 2-3

1 pack Quorn Sausages
1 red pepper
1 yellow pepper
2 tbsp olive oil
100g pasta shells
1 vegetable stock cube
4 tbsp good quality
red pesto
A handful of rocket leaves,
roughly chopped into
bite-size lengths

1. Brush the peppers with half of the oil and place under a hot grill. Cook until the skin is blackened and charred 10-15 minutes. Remove the skins, cores, seeds and cut into strips.

2. Cook the pasta according to pack instructions, crumbling the stock cube into the cooking water, drain and leave to cool.

3. With the remaining oil cook the Quorn Sausages according to pack instructions, cool and then slice diagonally.

4. Toss the sausages, pesto, pasta, peppers and rocket together, season to taste and serve immediately.

Hoisin Fillets with Zesty Citrus Salad

Preparation Time: 15 mins
Cooking Time: 15 mins
Serves: 4-6

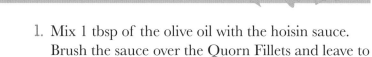

1 pack Quorn Fillets, defrosted*

4 tbsp olive oil

3 tbsp hoisin sauce

1 clove garlic, finely chopped

2 tbsp orange juice

1 tsp orange zest

200g long grain or brown rice

2 oranges, segmented

1 small red pepper, de-seeded and thinly sliced

1 small orange or yellow pepper, de-seeded and thinly sliced

150g courgette, cut into thin batons

4 spring onions, sliced diagonally into fine pieces

¾ cucumber, diced

2 tbsp parsley, finely chopped

2 tbsp mint, finely chopped plus extra for garnish

1 pack Italian or mixed salad leaves

1. Mix 1 tbsp of the olive oil with the hoisin sauce. Brush the sauce over the Quorn Fillets and leave to marinate for 10 minutes.

2. For the dressing, mix the remaining olive oil, garlic, orange juice and orange zest together in a bowl. Season to taste.

3. Cook the rice according to the pack instructions and keep warm.

4. Stir the dressing into the warm rice. Cover and leave to infuse and flavour the rice for 10 minutes. Add the remaining ingredients, apart from the salad leaves and fold through the rice. Cover and refrigerate until required.

5. Pre-heat the grill to a medium heat setting and place the marinated Quorn Fillets on a foil-lined baking tray. Cook for 3 minutes on each side until warmed through and sizzling.

6. Place the salad leaves on a serving platter or on individual plates. Arrange the rice salad over the salad leaves and top with the grilled, sticky hoisin Quorn Fillets.

Garnish with mint leaves and serve.

* for defrost instructions refer to page 166

Caesar Salad

Preparation Time: 10 mins
Cooking Time: 15 mins
Serves: 4

300g Quorn Chicken Style Pieces

100g Italian style hard cheese, grated plus extra shavings for garnish

Juice of 1 lemon

1 garlic clove

50ml white wine vinegar

1 free-range egg yolk

2 fillets of salted anchovies (optional)

200ml olive oil plus 2 tbsp extra for frying pieces

1 small loaf ciabatta bread

2 heads of cos or little gem lettuce (washed and dried)

1. To make dressing place the cheese, lemon juice, garlic clove, white wine vinegar and the egg yolk together with the anchovies (if using) in a blender and blend for 30 seconds.

2. With the blender still in motion, slowly add the olive oil until a smooth consistency is formed and season.

3. Pre-heat 1 tbsp of olive oil and fry the Quorn Pieces over a medium heat for approximately 10-15 minutes stirring continuously or until piping hot throughout.

4. Pre-heat grill to high, take the ciabatta bread and slice into quarter inch squares, place on baking sheet, drizzle with olive oil and grill until golden brown.

5. To assemble, take the cos lettuce, place in a large bowl, toss with the dressing and the Quorn Pieces and pile in the centre of your plates. Garnish with the ciabatta croutons and shavings of Italian style hard cheese. Serve.

Greek Style Salad

Preparation Time: 20 mins
Cooking Time: 6-7 mins
Serves: 4

300g Quorn Chicken Style Pieces, defrosted*

5 tbsp extra virgin olive oil

4 tbsp lemon juice, plus extra for squeezing

4 spring onions, sliced thinly

100g Feta cheese, crumbled

1 tbsp fresh mint, chopped

1 tsp dried oregano

2 romaine lettuce hearts, washed, dried and roughly torn

12 kalamata olives

4 tomatoes cut into wedges

2 ripe avocados, halved, stoned, peeled and sliced crossways

Half a small bunch of flat leaf parsley

1. Place the Quorn Pieces in a bowl with 1 tbsp each of olive oil and lemon juice then leave for 10 minutes to absorb the flavours. Fry over a medium heat to brown slightly for 6-7 minutes, set aside.

2. To make the dressing mix together the remaining olive oil and lemon juice, season to taste.

3. Combine the spring onions, Feta cheese, fresh mint and dried oregano and mix together with the dressing.

4. Make up the salad by layering the lettuce leaves on the bottom of a serving dish. Scatter over the Quorn Pieces then pour over the Feta dressing. Garnish with the olives, tomatoes and avocado. Squeeze on a little extra lemon juice. Pick the leaves off the parsley and scatter over the top.

Serve with fingers of warmed pitta bread.

* for defrost instructions refer to page 166

Thai
Noodles

Preparation Time: 15 mins
Cooking Time: 10 mins
Serves: 4

6 Quorn Fillets, defrosted*
1 tsp vegetable oil
60g bundle Thai
Rice Noodles
1 carrot, sliced into
thin strips
1 red pepper, de-seeded
and thinly sliced
4 spring onions, finely
sliced diagonally
200g beansprouts
1 tbsp fresh coriander,
finely chopped
1 tbsp fresh mint leaves

Dressing:
1 lime, grated zest
and juice
1-2 cloves garlic,
finely chopped
2 tsp soy sauce
2 tsp sweet chilli sauce
1 tbsp olive oil

1. Mix the dressing ingredients together and set aside.

2. Coat the Quorn Fillets lightly in the vegetable oil and dry-fry in a hot non-stick frying pan or hot griddle for 3 minutes on each side. Cook until hot and flecked with a dark golden brown colour. Slice diagonally and put into a large serving bowl. Pour the dressing over the Quorn Fillets and put to one side.

3. Cook the noodles according to pack instructions. Drain and refresh in cold water.

4. Fold the cooked noodles, salad vegetables and herbs through the Quorn Fillets and dressing. Adjust the seasoning to taste.

Serve at room temperature.

* for defrost instructions refer to page 166

Feta & Tomato
Ciabatta

Preparation Time: 5 mins
Cooking Time: 20 mins
Serves: 2

150g Frozen Quorn Chicken Style Pieces
1 tbsp olive oil
150g cherry tomatoes
100g mushrooms, quartered
2 garlic cloves, finely sliced
100g Feta cheese, cut into 1cm cubes
1-2 tbsp fresh basil leaves torn (optional)
1 large ciabatta loaf

1. Pre-heat oven to 200°C (400°F/Gas Mark 6).

2. In an ovenproof dish place the oil, tomatoes, mushrooms and Quorn Pieces, mix well to coat with the oil. Cook for 10 minutes.

3. Add the garlic and cook for a further 5 minutes before adding the Feta. Cook for a further 4-5 minutes until the cheese just begins to melt.

4. Whilst the Quorn mixture is cooking, warm the ciabatta as per the pack instructions.

5. To serve, slice the ciabatta loaf in half lengthways and top each half with the Quorn mixture, season with freshly ground black pepper and scatter over some torn basil. Alternatively divide the Quorn mixture into bowls, season, top with basil and serve with slices of warm ciabatta.

Super Duper Soups

For when a blanket
just won't do – our
super tasty soups
are sure to warm
you through.

Hearty Bean
& Pasta Soup

Preparation Time: 10 mins
Cooking Time: 30 mins
Serves: 4

175g Quorn Chicken
Style Pieces

1 tbsp vegetable oil

1 large onion, peeled
and finely chopped

2 cloves garlic, crushed

3 tbsp tomato purée

1 tbsp fresh
chopped rosemary

1 tsp marjoram

½ tsp thyme

400g tin chopped tomatoes

425g tin cannellini beans

1½ litres vegetable stock
made with 1 stock cube

½ tsp brown sugar

100g wholemeal
pasta shells

Italian style hard cheese,
freshly grated (optional)

1. Pre-heat the oil in a large saucepan, add the onions and cook for 5 minutes without colouring then add the garlic and cook for a further minute.

2. Now add the tomato purée, fresh rosemary, marjoram and thyme. Stir for a minute and add the chopped tomatoes, beans, stock, sugar and season to taste.

3. Bring to the boil, reduce the heat and cook for a further 10-12 minutes.

4. Then pour half the soup into a liquidiser and blend until completely smooth. Return the pureéd soup to the rest of the soup, add the Quorn Pieces and bring back to a simmer.

5. Add the pasta and cook for another 12-14 minutes stirring from time to time until the pasta is cooked.

Serve with grated cheese and fresh crusty bread.

Steak & Red
Pepper Broth

Preparation Time: 15 mins
Cooking Time: 12 mins
Serves: 4

300g Quorn Steak Strips

1½ tsp Chinese 5 spice powder

1 tbsp soy sauce

1 tbsp Schezuan sauce

1.2 litres hot vegetable stock

2½ cm piece fresh root ginger, finely chopped

2 cloves garlic, finely chopped

200g pak choi or spring cabbage, finely shredded

1 small red pepper, de-seeded and finely sliced

100g dried fine egg noodles, cooked and refreshed

4 spring onions, finely chopped

4 tbsp fresh flat leaf parsley, chopped

1. Put the Quorn Steak Strips in a bowl with the 5 Spice powder and shake together to coat evenly in the spices. Add the soy and Schezuan sauces, stir together, cover and leave to marinate.

2. Put the stock, ginger and garlic into a large saucepan. Bring to the boil, reduce the heat, cover and simmer for 5 minutes.

3. Add the pak choi, red pepper and the marinated Quorn Strips. Stir and simmer for 2-3 minutes. Stir in the noodles and cook for 2-3 minutes to heat through.

4. Just before serving, stir in half the spring onions and parsley. Spoon into bowls and garnish with the remaining spring onion and parsley. Serve immediately.

Spicy Coconut Noodle Soup

Preparation Time: 5 mins
Cooking Time: 10 mins
Serves: 4 as a starter or 2 as a lunch

Ingredients:

175g Quorn Chicken Style Pieces

2g dried mixed mushrooms (shiitake, oyster and porcini)

1 tbsp Thai red curry paste

400g tin reduced fat coconut milk

50g button mushrooms, sliced

60g dry Thai rice noodles, roughly broken, cooked according to back of pack instructions

100g beansprouts

50g fresh shiitake mushrooms, sliced

1 green chilli, sliced into fine rings

4 spring onions, finely shredded

1. Rehydrate the dried mushrooms in 250ml warm water for 30 minutes. Reserve the mushrooms and water.

2. Heat a large saucepan until hot. Dry-fry the curry paste, stirring constantly for 1 minute. Stir in the coconut milk, Quorn Pieces and the water from the dried mushrooms. Bring to the boil. Reduce the heat and simmer for 5 minutes.

3. Thinly slice the rehydrated mushrooms and button mushrooms and stir into the Quorn broth. Cook for 1 minute.

4. Add the noodles, beansprouts, fresh shiitake mushrooms, and most of the chilli and spring onions. Heat through for 1 minute.

5. Serve immediately in deep bowls and garnish with the remaining spring onion and chilli.

Cook's Tip: The fresh shiitake mushrooms spoil if cooked for too long.

Bacon & Sweetcorn Chowder

This is a quick chowder that's easy to make and a great supper.

Preparation Time: 5 mins
Cooking Time: 15 mins
Serves: 4

100g Quorn Smokey Bacon Style Slices, cut into small pieces
1 tbsp oil
1 small onion, finely chopped
350ml hot vegetable stock
1 large potato, peeled and diced into 1-2cm cubes
2 tsp cornflour
350ml semi-skimmed milk
175g frozen sweetcorn
Fresh chopped chives or parsley to garnish

1. Heat the oil in a large saucepan. Add the Quorn Smokey Bacon Style Slices and fry until they start to colour. Add the onion and fry for 3 minutes until soft but not coloured.

2. Stir in the hot stock and diced potato and bring up to the boil. Reduce the heat, cover and simmer for 5-6 minutes.

3. Mix the cornflour to a smooth paste with 2 tbsp of the milk. Pour the remaining milk and cornflour paste into the Quorn mixture. Return to a gentle simmer. Cook for 5 minutes or until the potato is tender, add the sweetcorn and heat through. Season to taste and stir in the fresh herbs.

Serve immediately with some crusty baguette.

Midweek
Winners

Who said easy can't be tasty?
This bounty of flavour-filled
recipes are quick to rustle up
and will definitely help get
you over the workday blues.

Pesto Crusted
Fillets

Preparation Time: 5 mins
Cooking Time: 14 mins
Serves: 3-4

1 pack Quorn Chicken Style Fillets
6 tsp green or red pesto
40g fresh ciabatta breadcrumbs
25g Italian hard cheese or
Cheddar, grated (optional)

1. Pre-heat oven to 200°C (400°F/Gas Mark 6) and lightly oil a baking tray.

2. Place Quorn Fillets on baking tray and and brush 1 tsp of the pesto over the top of each.

3. Sprinkle the ciabatta crumbs over the fillets and top with the grated cheese.

4. Bake on the middle shelf of the oven for 14 minutes, until the breadcrumbs are golden.

Steak Strips with Creamy Mustard Pasta

Preparation Time: 10 mins
Cooking Time: 15 mins
Serves: 4

300g Quorn Steak Strips or Quorn Chicken Style Pieces

150g dried penne pasta

1 tbsp light olive oil

2 shallots, peeled and finely chopped

2 cloves garlic, finely chopped

100g fine green beans, trimmed and blanched

175g frozen sweetcorn

150ml crème fraîche

1-2 tbsp wholegrain mustard

1 tsp lemon zest

2 tbsp chives

1. Bring a large pan of water to the boil and cook the pasta according to pack instructions.

2. Meanwhile, heat the oil in a frying pan and cook the Quorn Steak Strips or Pieces and shallots for 4 minutes. Add the garlic, beans and sweetcorn and cook for a further 3 minutes.

3. Mix the crème fraîche, mustard and lemon zest together in a bowl.

4. Drain the pasta and return to the pan over a medium heat, stir in the Quorn Steak Strips or Pieces and vegetable mixture. Add the flavoured crème fraîche and stir all the ingredients together. Warm through and season to taste.

Serve immediately topped with a sprinkling of chives.

Quorn Biriyani

A quick, easy and delicious recipe that's cooked in the microwave. Literally sit back and watch the magic. It's also great cold, as a salad.

Preparation Time: 10 mins
Cooking Time: 17 mins
Serves: 4

300g Quorn Chicken Style Pieces

3 tbsp of Tikka paste

250g Basmati rice

200g frozen mixed vegetables (peas, sweetcorn, peppers etc.)

1 red onion, finely diced

A good handful of dried apricots, diced

1 vegetable stock cube

600ml boiling water plus 3 tbsp extra

3 tbsp chopped coriander

Toasted flaked almonds to garnish

Instructions below are for an 800 watt power microwave.

1. Mix 2 tbsp of the Tikka paste with 3 tbsp of water, coat the Quorn Pieces well and reserve.

2. In a large microwaveable bowl add the rice, frozen mixed vegetables, red onion, diced apricots, 1 tbsp of Tikka paste and the crumbled stock cube. Pour over 600ml of boiling water and mix well, cover with cling film leaving a gap at the side to vent the steam, cook on high/full power for 6 minutes.

3. Peel back film and stir in the Quorn Pieces and any remaining marinade. Re-cover and cook for a further 6 minutes. Leave this now for 5 minutes to allow the rice to absorb all the liquid, then fluff up with a fork and stir through 2 tbsp of the chopped coriander.

4. Garnish with the remaining coriander and flaked almonds.

Serve with naan bread.

Hoisin
Noodles

Preparation Time: 20 mins
Cooking Time: 10 mins
Serves: 2

175g Quorn Steak Strips

2 blocks dried medium
egg noodles

1 tbsp vegetable oil

1 tbsp hoisin sauce

1 garlic clove, crushed

2 tbsp rice wine or
dry sherry

1 red chilli, de-seeded and
finely chopped

1 tbsp light soy sauce

50g mange tout, halved
lengthways

4 spring onions, trimmed
and chopped

75g beansprouts

125g pak choi, chopped

1. Cook the noodles as back of pack instructions. Drain and toss with vegetable oil.

2. Combine the Quorn Steak Strips, hoisin sauce, garlic, rice wine, chilli and soy sauce, mixing well. Heat a wok or stir-fry pan, then add the Quorn Steak Strips and stir-fry over a high heat for 3 minutes. Add the mange tout and half of the spring onions and stir-fry for a further 2 minutes.

3. Just before serving, stir in the beansprouts and pak choi into the Quorn Steak Strips, allowing the pak choi to wilt slightly. Fork in the noodles and serve immediately, garnish with remaining spring onions.

Quorn Pieces with Broccoli & Sweetcorn

The delicious combination of Quorn Pieces in a savoury sauce, accompanied with either pasta, noodles or potatoes, is sure to become a family favourite.

Preparation Time: 10 mins
Cooking Time: 15 mins
Serves: 4

300g Quorn Chicken Style Pieces

1 tbsp sunflower oil

1 medium onion, diced

2 cloves garlic, peeled and crushed

1 tsp Dijon mustard

75g button mushrooms, sliced

100g broccoli florets

100g sweetcorn

450ml semi-skimmed milk

1 vegetable stock cube

2 tbsp cornflour

25g mature Cheddar cheese, grated

1. Heat the oil in a large frying pan. Sauté the onion, garlic and Quorn Pieces for 1 minute. Stir in the mustard, mushrooms, broccoli, sweetcorn and sauté for 2 minutes.

2. Reserve 2 tbsp milk and crumble the stock cube into the rest, mix well. Pour the stock flavoured milk into the Quorn mixture, stir well and bring to the boil.

3. Mix the reserved milk and cornflour to a smooth paste. Pour into the Quorn mixture, stirring continuously until the sauce thickens. Season generously with black pepper. Remove from the heat.

4. Add the grated cheese and stir until just melted.

Quorn Spaghetti Bolognese

Preparation Time: 15 mins
Cooking Time: 30 mins
Serves: 4

350g Quorn Mince

2 tbsp olive oil

1 large onion, finely diced

1 large carrot, finely diced

1 stick celery, finely diced

2 garlic cloves, crushed

200g mushrooms, finely diced

400g tin chopped tomatoes

1 vegetable stock cube dissolved in 200ml boiling water

100ml red wine

1 tsp oregano

1 tsp marjoram

1 tbsp tomato purée

1 tbsp tomato ketchup

350g spaghetti (dried)

Hard cheese of your choice, grated to serve

1. Heat the oil in a large frying pan, add the onion, carrot, celery, garlic and cook over a medium heat stirring frequently for about 5 minutes until the vegetables have softened. Add the mushrooms and stir-fry for 2-3 minutes more.

2. Tip the tomatoes into the pan along with the vegetable stock, red wine, herbs, tomato purée and ketchup, stir well.

3. Cook over a low heat for 8-10 minutes until the vegetables are cooked.

4. Stir the Quorn Mince into the sauce, continue to cook over a low heat while you cook the spaghetti as per pack instructions. Season to taste.

5. Drain the spaghetti, spoon the Bolognese sauce on top and serve immediately.

Sprinkle generously with cheese.

"I use Quorn products all the time, and especially love how versatile the mince is. I have used it for cottage pie, Bolognese, chilli and home made burgers! I also love the pieces, they taste good in a stir-fry or a curry!"

Leah Foster, Quorn® lover since 2000

Chilli Con Quorn

Preparation Time: 10 mins
Cooking Time: 25 mins
Serves: 4

300g Quorn Mince
1 tbsp vegetable oil
1 large onion, chopped
2 cloves garlic, finely chopped
½ tsp ground cumin
1 tsp chilli powder
2 bay leaves
400g tin chopped tomatoes
300ml vegetable stock
1 green pepper, de-seeded and chopped
400g tin red kidney beans, drained
2 tsp cornflour
1 tbsp water

1. Heat the oil in a large saucepan. Fry the onion and garlic until soft and light golden brown. Add the Quorn Mince, spices and bay leaves, fry for 3 minutes.

2. Add the tomatoes, vegetable stock and green pepper and bring to the boil. Reduce the heat and simmer for 10 minutes, stirring occasionally.

3. Stir in the kidney beans and cook for 5 minutes.

4. Mix the cornflour with the water to a smooth paste. Stir into the Quorn chilli to thicken. Cook gently for a further 5 minutes. Remove the bay leaves and discard.

5. Serve immediately with jacket potato or boiled rice.

Accompany with tacos, crème fraîche and freshly chopped red chillies.

Lemon Chilli
Linguine

Preparation Time: 10 mins
Cooking Time: 15 mins
Serves: 4

300g Quorn Chicken Style Pieces
1 vegetable stock cube
225g dried linguine or spaghetti
1 tbsp olive oil
1 lemon zest and juice
1 large garlic clove finely chopped
1 red chilli, finely chopped
Freshly ground black pepper
3 tbsp fresh basil, finely shredded

1. In a large saucepan of boiling water, dissolve the stock cube and cook the linguine as per the pack instructions.

2. Meanwhile heat the oil in a frying pan, add the Quorn Pieces, pour over the lemon juice and fry for 5-6 minutes stirring frequently.

3. Add the garlic, red chilli and fry for a further 3 minutes stirring frequently.

4. Drain the linguine and add to the pan with the Quorn Pieces, add the lemon zest and season well with black pepper. Stir through the basil and serve.

Beef
Teriyaki

Preparation Time: 10 mins + 30 mins marinating
Cooking Time: 15 mins
Serves: 4

300g Quorn Steak Strips or Quorn Chicken Style Pieces

2 tbsp vegetable oil

2 tbsp tamari soy sauce or teriyaki sauce

1 clove garlic, finely chopped

1 tbsp ginger, grated

½ orange, juice and zest

2 tbsp rice wine vinegar

125g dried egg noodles

½ red pepper, thinly sliced

50g mushrooms, thinly sliced

6 spring onions, sliced diagonally into 1 cm pieces

Juice of ½ lemon

2 tbsp coriander, finely chopped plus extra for garnish

1. Place the Quorn Strips or Pieces into a bowl and add 1 tbsp of the vegetable oil, the soy sauce, garlic, ginger, orange juice and zest and rice wine vinegar. Leave to marinate for 30 minutes.

2. Cook the egg noodles according to pack instructions.

3. Place a wok over a high heat, pour in the remaining tbsp of oil and fry the red pepper for 2 minutes then add the mushrooms and spring onion and cook for a further 2 minutes.

4. Add the Quorn Strips or Pieces and the marinade to the wok and stir-fry for 6 minutes then add the lemon juice and coriander.

5. Lastly add the noodles and combine in the wok with the other ingredients, stir-fry for a further 4 minutes.

Serve immediately with a sprinkling of coriander.

Quorn Steak Supper in a Flash

Preparation Time: 10 mins
Cooking Time: 10 mins
Serves: 4

175g Quorn Steak Strips or Quorn Beef or Quorn Chicken Style Pieces

25g flour

1 tsp paprika

1 tbsp vegetable oil

1 red onion, finely sliced

175g new potatoes, cooked and halved

2-3 cloves garlic, finely chopped

100g cherry or baby plum tomatoes, halved

300ml hot vegetable stock

Dash of vegetarian Worcestershire sauce

2 tbsp chopped parsley

1. Mix the flour and paprika together in a bowl, season to taste. Add the Quorn Steak Strips or Pieces and shake all the ingredients together to fully coat with the seasoned flour.

2. Heat the oil in a non-stick frying pan and fry the Quorn Strips or Pieces for 2-3 minutes until they brown. Add the onion and cooked potatoes and continue to stir fry for 3 minutes until the onions soften and the potatoes begin to colour. Stir in the garlic and tomatoes and fry for 2 minutes.

3. Add the stock and Worcestershire sauce and stir together. Adjust the seasoning if required.

4. Sprinkle the chopped parsley over the dish just before serving.

Serve immediately accompanied with garlic bread.

Pizza Topped Burgers

Preparation Time: 5 mins
Cooking Time: 10 mins
Serves: 2

4 Quorn Burgers
2 muffins, cut in half
2 tsp good quality red or green pesto
1 fresh tomato, thinly sliced
1 tbsp basil leaves, torn
50g Cheddar or Mozzarella, grated or sliced

1. Grill the Quorn Burgers according to instructions on pack.

2. Toast the muffins under the grill until lightly browned.

3. Spoon ½ tsp of pesto over each muffin half, place burger on top. Top with slices of tomato and the torn basil leaves. Divide the cheese between the burgers and brown under a hot grill until the cheese is golden and bubbling.

Serve with a fresh mixed salad and crispy potato skins.

Comforting
Classics

Want a cuddle on a plate?
This range of feel good food
is sure to do just that - and
taste great too!

Quorn Lasagne

Preparation Time: 15 mins
Cooking Time: 35 mins
Serves: 4

300g Quorn Mince
1 tbsp olive oil
1 onion, finely diced
2 cloves garlic, crushed
100g mushrooms, diced
400g passata
3 tbsp red pesto
1 tsp dried oregano
3 tbsp red wine - fruity red
½ tsp sugar
1 vegetable stock cube
2 tbsp fresh basil leaves, torn
8 lasagne sheets

Cheese sauce:
25g butter
25g plain flour
300ml semi-skimmed milk
100g mature Cheddar cheese, grated

1. Pre-heat the oven to 200°C (400°F/Gas Mark 6). Heat the oil in the pan and fry the onion and garlic for 5 minutes until softened. Add the diced mushrooms and cook for a further 2-3 minutes.

2. Stir in the Quorn Mince and then add the passata, red pesto, oregano, wine, sugar and vegetable stock cube. Gently simmer for 8 minutes. Season to taste and stir in the basil. Remove from the heat.

3. Meanwhile, make the cheese sauce by melting the butter in a pan and slowly stir in the flour. Slowly add the milk stirring continuously to avoid lumps, until it thickens. Stir in three quarters of the grated cheese, keeping the remainder for the top of the lasagne.

4. To assemble the dish, put 2 pasta sheets in the base of a lightly greased shallow ovenproof dish. Spoon a third of the mixture on the lasagne sheets. Repeat these layers finishing with a layer of lasagne. Pour over the cheese sauce, scatter over the remaining cheese and bake in the oven for 25 minutes until the top is golden brown and bubbling.

Serve with fresh green salad and garlic bread.

Toad in the Hole with Red Onion & Thyme Batter

A subtle twist on an old favourite. Delicious served with rich vegetable gravy and fresh seasonal vegetables.

Preparation Time: 10 mins
Cooking Time: 60 mins
Serves: 2-3

1 pack Quorn Sausages
1 red onion, cut into wedges
1 tbsp olive oil
175g plain flour, sifted
2 free-range eggs
300ml milk
2 tsp wholegrain mustard
1 tbsp fresh thyme leaves or 1½ tsp dried thyme

1. Pre-heat the oven to 200°C (400°F/ Gas Mark 6). Put the onion wedges, oil and sausages into a small, shallow non-stick tin and roast for 20 minutes.

2. Prepare the batter by sifting the flour into a bowl, drop the eggs into the centre and beat these along with the milk a little at a time until it makes a smooth batter. Stir in the mustard, thyme and season to taste.

3. Pour the batter into the tin with the onions and sausages and return to the oven for 40 minutes until the batter has risen and turned golden.

Quorn Cottage Pie

Preparation Time: 15 mins
Cooking Time: 30 mins
Serves: 4

300g of Quorn Mince

Topping:
700g potatoes, peeled and roughly chopped
225g parsnip, peeled and chopped
2 tbsp milk

Filling:
1 tbsp vegetable oil
1 medium onion, finely chopped
1 medium carrot, finely chopped
100g frozen peas or mixed vegetables
400ml vegetable stock
1 tbsp vegetarian Worcestershire sauce
1 tbsp tomato purée
2 tbsp reduced salt soy sauce
1 tbsp cornflour mixed to paste with 1 tbsp cold water

1. Pre-heat oven to 180°C (350°F/Gas Mark 4).

2. Boil the potatoes and parsnip until tender. Drain and set aside.

3. Meanwhile heat the oil in a large pan, add the onion and the carrot and fry gently until the onions are soft.

4. Add the Quorn Mince, frozen vegetables, vegetable stock, Worcestershire sauce, tomato purée, soy sauce and season to taste. Simmer ingredients together for 5 minutes. Add the cornflour paste and simmer gently until the sauce thickens then place in an ovenproof dish.

5. Mash the potatoes and parsnip with the milk until smooth, season to taste. Place the topping over the Quorn filling and fluff up with a fork.

6. Bake for 20 minutes or until the topping is golden and crisp.

Serve immediately with a selection of fresh seasonal vegetables.

Leek Pie with Quorn Pieces

Preparation Time: 10 mins + 30 mins chilling
Cooking Time: 25 mins
Serves: 4

300g Quorn Chicken Style Pieces

Pastry:

150g plain flour + extra for dusting

¼ tsp mustard powder

50g butter, diced

75g Wensleydale cheese, grated

5-6 tbsp chilled water

Filling:

40g butter

1 tsp vegetable oil

2 medium leeks sliced

2 cloves garlic, finely chopped

25g plain flour

½ tsp mustard powder

1 vegetable stock cube dissolved in 100ml boiling water

200ml semi-skimmed milk plus extra for glazing

1. Pre-heat the oven to 200°C (400°F/Gas Mark 6).

2. For the pastry, mix the flour and mustard powder together. Rub in the butter until the mixture resembles fine breadcrumbs. Add the grated cheese and stir through.

3. Gradually add sufficient water to form a firm dough. Cover with cling film and chill for 30 minutes.

4. For the filling, melt the butter and oil in a large saucepan. Add the leeks and cook for 5 minutes over a medium heat until softened but not coloured. Stir in the garlic and Quorn Pieces and continue to cook for 2 minutes.

5. Stir in the flour and mustard powder and cook for 1 minute. Gradually add the stock and milk, stirring until the sauce thickens. Season to taste. Spoon the Quorn mixture into a pie dish. Cover with cling film and cool.

6. Roll out the pastry on a lightly floured surface and use to cover the top of the pie dish. Brush the pastry with a little milk to glaze.

7. Bake for 25 minutes until the top is golden brown.

Serve with seasonal vegetables and new potatoes.

Steak, Ale & Mushroom Pie

Preparation Time: 15 mins
Cooking Time: 35 mins
Serves: 4

300g Quorn Beef Style Pieces or Quorn Steak Strips

1 tbsp olive oil

1 small onion, finely chopped

1 carrot, thinly sliced

1 stick celery, thinly sliced

250g mushrooms, sliced (Portabello are best if you can get them)

1 garlic clove, crushed

½ tsp brown sugar

1½ tsp cornflour

100ml pale ale

1 vegetable stock cube

1 generous tsp tomato purée

½ tsp yeast extract

½ tsp dried thyme

½ tsp dried rosemary

220g puff pastry for top of pie

1 free-range egg to glaze

1. Pre-heat oven to 200°C (400°F/Gas Mark 6).

2. Heat oil in a frying pan, add the onion, carrot and celery and fry gently for 2-3 minutes until softened and starting to brown, then add the mushrooms and the garlic and continue to cook for a further 3 minutes until the mushrooms have softened. Toss in the Quorn Pieces or Steak Strips and stir all of these ingredients together.

3. Add the brown sugar and cornflour and continue to cook gently for 1 minute. Add the pale ale, crumbled stock cube, tomato purée, yeast extract, and herbs.

4. Simmer gently for 5 minutes until the sauce is thickened and bubbling. Season to taste. If the sauce is a little too thick, add 2 tbsp of water.

5. Place the steak and mushroom filling into an ovenproof dish, moisten the edges of the dish with a little beaten egg, cover with puff pastry, trim the edges and glaze with a little more beaten egg and pop into the oven for 20 minutes until the pastry is golden.

Serve with a selection of seasonal vegetables of your choice.

Sweet
Potato Loaf

Preparation Time: 20 mins
Cooking Time: 45 mins
Serves: 6

125g Quorn Mince
70g bulgur wheat
2 tbsp olive oil
100g carrot, grated
1 small onion, grated
100g sweet potato, grated
2 cloves garlic, finely chopped
70g pinhead oatmeal or rolled oats
1½ tsp yeast extract
70ml vegetable stock made with 1 stock cube
1 large free-range egg, beaten
1½ tsp fresh thyme, leaves only, chopped
½ tsp white pepper
1 sprig of rosemary

1. Pre-heat oven to 200°C (400°F/Gas Mark 6).

2. Cook the bulgar wheat according to the instructions on the back of packet.

3. Heat the oil in a frying pan and fry the grated vegetables and garlic for 3 minutes.

4. Put the Quorn Mince into a large mixing bowl. Add the fried vegetables, cooked bulgar wheat, oats, yeast extract, vegetable stock, egg, thyme and white pepper. Mix together well and season to taste.

5. Line a 900g loaf tin with greaseproof paper. Place the sprig of rosemary in the bottom of the tin and spoon the Quorn mixture over the top, pressing the ingredients down firmly. Cover with foil. Bake in a hot oven for 40 minutes.

6. Rest the Quorn roast for 5 minutes before turning out and slicing.

Accompany hot with roasted vegetables and a spicy sauce or cold with onion chutney.

Quorn Fillets in Red Pesto Sauce

Rustle up a bowl of cooked tagliatelle or some warm ciabatta bread to accompany this easy supper dish! Perfect for impromptu entertaining.

Preparation Time: 20 mins
Cooking Time: 20 mins
Serves: 2-3

6 Quorn Fillets or 300g Quorn Pieces
2 tbsp olive oil
100ml vegetable stock
2 tbsp tomato purée
2 tbsp good quality red pesto
1 tsp fresh thyme, chopped
3 tbsp half fat crème fraîche
Basil leaves, to garnish

1. Heat the oil in a shallow pan and lightly brown the Quorn Fillets or Pieces.

2. In a bowl mix together the stock, tomato purée, pesto and thyme. Pour over the fillets or pieces. Cover and simmer for 10 minutes.

3. Transfer the fillets or pieces to warmed plates. Stir the crème fraîche into the sauce, add seasoning to taste and spoon over the fillets or pieces. Garnish with freshly torn basil.

Lazy
Weekend
Recipes

Classic recipes that you
can take time to enjoy
creating, as well as eating.

Spanish Style Casserole

Preparation Time: 10 mins
Cooking Time: 25 mins
Serves: 4

300g Quorn Sausages
2 tbsp olive oil
2 onions, thinly sliced
2 garlic cloves, crushed
1 red pepper, de-seeded and diced
1 green pepper, de-seeded and diced
100g sweetcorn
1 tsp smoked paprika
2 tsp mild chilli powder
100ml apple juice
400g tin chopped tomatoes
150ml vegetable stock
400g tin cannelloni beans or broad beans, drained
1 small bunch of flat leaf parsley, finely chopped

1. Heat 1tbsp of the oil in a large frying pan and fry the Quorn Sausages for 2-3 minutes until lightly browned. Remove from the pan and set aside to cool then slice diagonally into 5 pieces.

2. Add the remaining oil to the pan and fry the onions and garlic for 4-5 minutes or until softened, then add the peppers and continue frying for 3-4 minutes. A little extra stock or water will prevent sticking if needed.

3. Stir in the sweetcorn, paprika and chilli powder and cook for 2 more minutes before adding the apple juice.

4. Pour in the tomatoes, stock, add the beans and sliced sausages, season to taste.

5. Cover and simmer for 10 minutes before sprinkling with parsley.

Vegetable
Paella

Preparation Time: 10 mins
Cooking Time: 40 mins
Serves: 4

300g Quorn Sausages, defrosted* if using frozen

2 tbsp olive oil

1 onion, thinly sliced

2 garlic cloves, crushed

1 red pepper, de-seeded and sliced

1 yellow pepper, de-seeded and sliced

400g fresh tomatoes, skinned and chopped

200g thin green beans, cut into bite-sized pieces

200g peas

250g long grain rice

1½ tsp smoked paprika

½ tsp saffron

1 tsp turmeric

1 tsp mild chilli powder

Zest of 1 lemon

1 tbsp lemon juice

700ml vegetable stock

3 tbsp parsley, chopped

1. Warm a pan and heat 1 tbsp oil. Cut each Quorn Sausage into bite-sized chunks and fry until golden 3-4 minutes, set aside.

2. Gently fry the onions and garlic in the remaining oil until soft and golden. Add the peppers and fry for a further 4-5 minutes. Stir in the tomatoes, beans and peas and cook for 6 minutes.

3. Add the rice, paprika, saffron, turmeric, chilli, lemon zest and juice, stir well.

4. Stir in the stock and simmer for about 15 minutes. Stir in the sausage pieces and continue simmering for a further 5-10 minutes or until the rice is tender, adding more liquid if required.

5. Season to taste, sprinkle over the parsley and serve.

for defrost instructions refer to page 166

unch
Frittata

Preparation Time: 10 mins
Cooking Time: 20 mins
Serves: 2-3

4 Quorn Sausages

2 tbsp olive oil

1-2 shallots, peeled
and thinly sliced

1 medium potato, peeled,
boiled and roughly diced
into 1cm cubes (optional)

50g button mushrooms,
halved

4 plum or cherry
tomatoes, halved

4 large free-range eggs

1 tbsp water

Good pinch paprika
(optional)

2-3 tbsp fresh flat leaf
parsley, chopped

1. Heat the oil in a large non-stick frying pan (approx. 26 cm diameter). Fry the Quorn Sausages for 8 minutes, add the shallots and diced potato and continue cooking for 3-4 minutes on a medium heat until golden brown. Remove the Quorn Sausages and slice diagonally into bite-sized pieces. Return to the pan.

2. Add the mushrooms and tomatoes and fry for 2 minutes.

3. Lightly whisk the eggs, water, paprika and seasoning together in a bowl. Stir in the parsley.

4. Pour the egg mixture into the frying pan and lightly shake the pan to distribute the mixture. Reduce the heat a little and cook the bottom of the frittata for 2-3 minutes until lightly set.

5. Place the pan under a hot grill and finish off the cooking for about 2-3 minutes until the egg mixture is just set.

6. Leave to stand for 1-2 minutes before serving and dust the top with a little extra paprika.

Serve with fresh crusty bread.

Quorn Bolognese
Pizza

Preparation Time: 5 mins
Cooking Time: 20-25 mins
Serves: 2

175g Quorn Mince
1 tbsp vegetable oil
1 small red onion, thinly sliced
1 clove of garlic, crushed
200g tin chopped tomatoes
2 tbsp tomato purée
1½ tsp dried oregano
1 vegetable stock cube
1 x large pizza base (30cm) or
2 x small pizza bases (15cm)
50g Mozzarella, grated
50g Cheddar, grated

1. Pre-heat the oven to 200°C (400°F/Gas Mark 6).

2. Pre-heat the oil in a pan and fry the onion and garlic gently to soften 4-5 minutes. Add the tomatoes, Quorn Mince, tomato purée, 1 tsp of the oregano and crumble in the stock cube. Bring to the boil and simmer for 5 minutes. Season to taste.

3. Place pizza base(s) onto a baking tray and top with the Quorn Mince mixture, sprinkle over the remaining oregano and top with the cheeses. Bake for 10-15 minutes until cheese is golden brown and bubbling.

Quorn Balls in Tomato Sauce

Preparation Time: 10 mins
Cooking Time: 30-40 mins
Serves: 4

1 pack Quorn Balls –
any variety

2 tbsp light olive oil

1 onion, finely chopped

2 cloves garlic, finely chopped

1 small carrot, finely chopped

400g tin chopped tomatoes

300ml hot vegetable stock

¼ tsp dried oregano

2 bay leaves

A handful of fresh
basil leaves, torn

4 tsp grated
Parmesan cheese

1. Heat the oil in a large saucepan and fry the onion, garlic and carrot for 7 minutes over a low heat until soft but not coloured.

2. Add the tomatoes, stock, oregano, bay leaves and bring slowly to the boil, stirring occasionally.

3. Add the Quorn Balls and stir into the sauce. Cover, reduce the heat and simmer for 20-30 minutes to reduce and thicken the sauce. Remove the bay leaves and discard. Season to taste.

4. Add most of the basil and stir into the sauce. Serve in bowls garnished with grated Parmesan and a little torn basil.

Accompany with penne, spaghetti or other favourite pasta shape.

103

"I keep my freezer full of Quorn products. They are the mainstay of my diet. I have them at barbecues, for breakfast, lunch and dinner. Thanks for your products."

Lecia Holston, Quorn® lover since 2004

Carbonara with Quorn Mince

Preparation Time: 10 mins
Cooking Time: 10 mins
Serves: 4

175g Quorn Mince

100g Quorn Deli Ham or Quorn Bacon Rashers, chopped

350g spaghetti

1 tbsp olive oil

1 shallot, finely chopped

1 clove of garlic, finely chopped

3 medium free-range eggs, whisked

1 tbsp Parmesan or vegetarian medium fat hard cheese

Handful chopped, fresh parsley

1. Bring a large pan of water to the boil and add the spaghetti, cook as per pack instructions.

2. Meanwhile, heat the olive oil in a medium-sized pan over a moderate heat. Add the shallot, garlic and the Quorn Mince, sauté for 3 minutes. Stir in the ham or bacon and cook for a further 2 minutes. Season to taste.

3. Whisk the eggs in a large serving bowl with the grated Parmesan. Drain the cooked spaghetti, reserving 2 large spoonfuls of the cooking water.

4. Add the spaghetti to the whisked eggs in the serving bowl with the ham and mince mixture and the reserved cooking water. Keep stirring until all the ingredients are well combined. Divide the pasta between 4 serving bowls and serve with some freshly ground black pepper and garnish with the parsley.

Pasta Carbonara

Preparation Time: 5 mins
Cooking Time: 20 mins
Serves: 2

100g of Quorn Deli Ham or Quorn Deli Bacon cut into thin strips or diced (you could also use Quorn Bacon Style Bits)

1 tbsp vegetable oil

175g dried spaghetti

2 free-range eggs

2-3 heaped tbsp of vegetarian Italian style hard cheese plus extra for garnish

2 tbsp crème fraîche

Pinch of grated nutmeg

1 tbsp parsley, chopped

1. Pre-heat the oil in a frying pan and fry the Quorn Deli Ham or Deli Bacon over a medium heat for 3 minutes.

2. Plunge the spaghetti into a large saucepan of boiling water and cook as per pack instructions.

3. Meanwhile, in a small bowl whisk together the eggs, the Italian hard cheese, crème fraîche, nutmeg, parsley and season to taste.

4. Drain the spaghetti reserving 2 tbsp of the cooking water, return to the pan, add the Quorn Deli Ham or Deli Bacon and the cooking liquid, mixing together.

5. Stir in the egg mixture, using a fork to lift the spaghetti so it is evenly coated.

Serve immediately with a little extra cheese and freshly ground black pepper.

Pizza with Quorn Italian **Balls**

Preparation Time: 5 mins
Cooking Time: 15 mins
Serves: 4

200g Quorn Balls, defrosted* if using frozen
1 large ready-rolled pizza base
200g fresh tomato pizza sauce
150g Mozzarella cheese, cut into small dice
50g mixed grated Cheddar and Mozzarella cheese
1 tsp dried oregano
Ground black pepper
2 tbsp olive oil (optional)
Black olives (optional)

1. Pre-heat the oven to 220°C (425°F/Gas Mark 7).

2. Meanwhile place the pizza base on an oven tray and spread over the tomato sauce, leaving the outer rim uncovered. Sprinkle evenly with the diced Mozzarella. Cut the Quorn Balls into quarters and place the pieces evenly over the pizza base. Then lastly cover with the grated cheeses.

3. Sprinkle with oregano, ground black pepper, olive oil and olives. Place the pizza in the pre-heated oven. Bake for 10-15 minutes or until the crust is golden brown and the cheese is bubbling.

for defrost instructions refer to page 166

Quorn Fillets
Provençale

Preparation Time: 10 mins
Cooking Time: 30 mins
Serves: 3-4

6 Quorn Fillets, defrosted*

1 tbsp herbes de Provençe

4 tbsp olive oil

1 large onion, finely chopped

2 cloves of garlic, finely chopped

1 red, green and yellow pepper, de-seeded and cut into wide strips

2 medium courgettes, sliced

400g tin chopped tomatoes

1 vegetable stock cube

2 tbsp fresh parsley, chopped

1. Mix the herbes de Provençe into 2 tbsp of the olive oil and rub over the Quorn Fillets, set aside until needed.

2. Heat 1 tbsp of the oil in a deep frying pan. Add the onions, garlic, peppers, courgettes and cover. Gently cook for 10 minutes, or until the vegetables are softened, stir occasionally. Add the tomatoes, stock cube and cover. Simmer for a further 10 minutes, season to taste and then stir in the parsley.

3. Meanwhile, in a non-stick frying pan heat the remaining oil and cook the fillets for 5 to 6 minutes over a medium to high heat until golden brown.

4. Remove lid from vegetables, place fillets on the top of the vegetables and simmer for a further 2-3 minutes.

Garnish with basil leaves and serve with crusty bread.

* for defrost instructions refer to page 166

Vegetable
Mince Curry

When time is short this is a delicious, speedy curry.

Preparation Time: 10 mins
Cooking Time: 25 mins
Serves: 4

300g Quorn Mince

1 large potato, peeled and cut into bite-sized chunks

175g cauliflower, cut into small florets (optional)

1 350-425g jar curry sauce – Madras works well

175g peas, frozen

2 handfuls fresh baby spinach leaves

1. Cook the potatoes and cauliflower in boiling water for 8-10 minutes.

2. Pour the curry sauce into a large saucepan and heat gently.

3. Add the Quorn Mince, potato and cauliflower. Bring to the boil, reduce the heat and simmer for 10 minutes.

4. Add the green vegetables and cook for a further 2-3 minutes. Season to taste.

Serve the curry with naan bread and mango chutney.

Quorn Moussaka

Preparation Time: 10 mins
Cooking Time: 50 mins
Serves: 4-6

350g Quorn Mince
3 tbsp olive oil
1 large onion, chopped
2 cloves garlic,
finely chopped
1 large carrot, finely diced
100g puy lentils
canned (optional)
390g carton
chopped tomatoes
2 tsp dried oregano
1 tsp ground allspice
or cinnamon
2 bay leaves
1 tsp dried mint
1 large aubergine,
thinly sliced

For the topping:
410g tin evaporated milk
40g cornflour
25g butter
25g plain flour
Pinch grated nutmeg
1 free-range egg, beaten
50g grated Cheddar
cheese

1. Pre-heat the oven to 180°C (350°F/Gas Mark 4).

2. Heat 2 tbsp of the oil in a heavy base saucepan. Add the onion, garlic and carrots and fry for 5 minutes until soft and lightly coloured. Add the Quorn Mince, tomatoes, oregano, allspice or cinnamon, bay leaves and mint. Bring to the boil, reduce the heat, cover and simmer for 10 minutes, stirring occasionally. Season to taste.

3. Brush the aubergine slices on both sides with the remaining oil and grill on both sides until brown. Lay the aubergine slices on absorbent kitchen paper. Set aside.

4. For the sauce, pour the evaporated milk into a measuring jug and make up to 1 litre with water. Mix the cornflour to a smooth paste with 6 tbsp of the milk and set aside.

5. Melt the butter in a saucepan, stir in the plain flour and cook over a low heat for 2 minutes. Gradually blend in the milk and water mix and slowly bring to the boil, stirring constantly. Reduce the heat and simmer for 3 minutes. Stir in the cornflour paste and continue to cook over a low heat until the sauce thickens. Remove from the heat and add the nutmeg. Season to taste and stir in the beaten egg.

6. Arrange the mince and aubergine slices in layers in a large baking dish. Remove the bay leaves and discard. Cover with the sauce, sprinkle with grated cheese.

7. Bake, uncovered, in a hot oven for about 30 minutes until the top is a rich golden brown and the dish is piping hot.

Savoury Carrot
Burgers

Preparation Time: 15 mins
Cooking Time: 12 mins
Serves: 4

175g Quorn Mince

5 medium carrots, sliced and cooked until soft then drained

1 level tsp yeast extract

50g fresh wholemeal bread crumbs (2 slices approx)

6 dried apricots, finely chopped

50g sultanas, finely chopped

4 spring onions, finely sliced including green part

1 tsp dried chilli flakes

1 orange, zest only, finely grated

2 tbsp fresh parsley, finely chopped

2 tbsp fresh mint, finely chopped

1 tbsp fresh rosemary, finely chopped

1 medium free-range egg, beaten

Vegetable oil for frying

Little flour to dust burgers

Burger buns/pitta bread, garlic mayonnaise and salad leaves to serve

1. Mash the carrots while still warm and stir through the yeast extract so that it melts.

2. Add all the remaining ingredients and mix well. Season to taste.

3. Form the burgers either with your hands or use a suitably-sized pastry cutter as a mould. Pack the mixture firmly into the mould and remove carefully. This mixture makes 10-12 burgers depending on the size.

4. Dust the burgers lightly with flour, shallow fry in pre-heated oil for 10-12 minutes on a medium heat, turning halfway for even browning. Drain on kitchen paper.

Serve in a bun or a warmed pitta bread with a little garlic mayonnaise and crispy lettuce leaves.

Mexican
Fajitas

Preparation Time: 5 mins + 30 mins marinating
Cooking Time: 10 mins
Serves: 4

300g Quorn Chicken
Style Pieces

1 lime, zest and juice

1 tbsp dried oregano

½ tsp cayenne pepper

½ tsp cinnamon

½ tsp ground cumin

½ tsp caster sugar

1 tbsp vegetable oil

1 onion, finely sliced

1 red, green and yellow
pepper, de-seeded and
finely sliced

1 tbsp fresh coriander

1 pack soft flour tortillas
(8 to a pack)

Fresh tomato salsa, soured
cream or guacamole
to serve

1. Mix the lime zest and juice with the oregano, spices, sugar and season. Add the Quorn Pieces, mix well and set aside to marinate for 30 minutes.

2. Pre-heat the oil in a large frying pan or wok, stir-fry the onions and peppers for 3-4 minutes over a medium heat. Add the Quorn Pieces and any remaining marinade and continue to stir-fry for 5-6 minutes over a medium to high heat. Just before serving stir through the fresh coriander.

3. Prepare the tortillas following the pack instructions.

4. To serve, spread a little salsa over the warm tortilla, top with the Quorn mixture and a dollop of soured cream or guacamole, fold the tortilla over the filling and serve immediately.

Food with
Friends

Flavour-filled dishes,
ideal for group gatherings
around the table and
perfect for everyone to
tuck into.

Tortilla Stack

Preparation Time: 10 mins
Cooking Time: 30 mins
Serves: 4

300g Quorn Mince

1 small onion, peeled and finely chopped

1 large garlic clove, peeled and finely chopped

2 tsp ground paprika

1 tsp mild chilli powder

400g chopped tomatoes

2 tbsp tomato purée

1 tbsp vegetarian Worcestershire or brown sauce

3 tbsp freshly chopped coriander leaves

4-6 flour tortillas

200g mature Cheddar cheese, grated

1. Pre-heat the oven to 200°C (400°F/Gas Mark 6).

2. Heat a large, shallow, non-stick frying pan until hot and cook the onion and garlic for 5 minutes. Then add the Quorn Mince, paprika, chilli powder, chopped tomatoes, tomato purée, Worcestershire or brown sauce. Season to taste.

3. Simmer for 10-15 minutes. Stir through the coriander.

4. Place a tortilla on a large non-stick baking tray and spoon over a portion of the mince mixture evenly and a handful of cheese. Repeat with the remaining ingredients and top with the remaining cheese.

5. Bake for 10 minutes or until the cheese melts. Cut into quarters and serve with salad leaves.

Gnocchi Bake

Preparation Time: 10 mins
Cooking Time: 20-25 mins
Serves: 2-3

100g Quorn Deli Ham/
Smoky Ham (or Quorn
Deli Bacon) sliced into
long strips

25g butter

25g plain flour

300ml semi-skimmed milk

100g half-fat Cheddar
cheese, grated

1 pack of fresh gnocchi
(packs size vary between
400g or 500g)

225g baby leaf spinach
(ready washed)

Pinch of grated nutmeg

1. Pre-heat the oven to 190°C (375°F/Gas Mark 5), lightly grease an ovenproof dish.

2. Melt the butter in a saucepan, add the flour, cook for 1 minute stirring continuously, gradually add the milk, slowly bring to the boil stirring. Simmer for 2 minutes stirring until thickened, add three quarters of the cheese and season to taste.

3. Cook the gnocchi following the pack instructions. To wilt the spinach place into a colander and when the gnocchi is cooked drain the water through the spinach.

4. Put the gnocchi and spinach into the ovenproof dish, season with freshly ground black pepper and a pinch of grated nutmeg, stir through the Quorn Deli strips.

5. Pour over the cheese sauce and top with the remaining grated cheese, bake in the oven for 15 to 20 minutes until the cheese is bubbling and golden.

Serve with a glass of wine, a chunk of warmed ciabatta and salad leaves.

Tarragon Fillets in Vermouth

Preparation Time: 5 mins
Cooking Time: 25 mins
Serves: 4

1 packet Quorn Fillets

2 tbsp vegetable oil

1 leek, finely sliced

100g chestnut mushrooms, finely sliced

1 tbsp fresh chopped tarragon or
1 tsp dried tarragon

100ml white Vermouth

300ml hot vegetable stock

200ml crème fraîche (full or half-fat)

1 tbsp fresh chopped parsley

1. Lightly sauté the Quorn Fillets in half the oil in a shallow frying pan for 5-6 minutes or until golden on each side. Take out and set aside.

2. Add the remaining oil to the pan and sauté the leeks gently for 3-4 minutes or until soft, then add the mushrooms and continue cooking for 2 minutes.

3. Put the fillets back in the pan and add the tarragon and Vermouth, simmer for 4-5 minutes until it has evaporated by half and then add the stock and continue to simmer for 5 minutes. Season to taste.

4. Stir in the crème fraîche and serve immediately sprinkled with fresh parsley accompanied by a selection of fresh vegetables, new potatoes or boiled rice.

"My favourite is sausage and mushroom sandwiches – Saturday mornings wouldn't be the same without them! I have introduced my sister to Quorn Sausages and Quorn Mince and she now eats them instead of meat ones, as she likes to know that they are healthier."

Sally Hiscock, Quorn® lover since 1985

Italian Balls in Blue Cheese Sauce

Preparation Time: 5 mins
Cooking Time: 30 mins
Serves: 4

300g Quorn Balls

1 tbsp oil

40g butter or margarine

40g plain flour

250ml vegetable stock

250ml milk

75g crumbled Gorgonzola cheese (Roquefort or Stilton are tasty alternatives)

Pinch of freshly grated nutmeg

Zest of half a lemon

1 tbsp freshly chopped parsley

1. Pre-heat the oven to 180°C (350°F/Gas Mark 4).

2. Heat the oil and gently cook the Quorn Balls in a shallow frying pan for 5 minutes.

3. Melt the butter or margarine in a small heavy-based saucepan, add the flour, stir well and heat gently for 1 minute. Add the vegetable stock and milk gradually and continue stirring over the heat until the sauce has thickened.

4. Reduce the heat and add the crumbled Gorgonzola, nutmeg, lemon zest and season to taste. Continue to simmer gently for a further 4 minutes stirring regularly.

5. Place the balls in an ovenproof dish and pour over the Gorgonzola sauce. Bake in the oven for 15-20 minutes or until golden brown and bubbling. Sprinkle with parsley before serving.

Fantastic served over pasta or with some fresh crusty bread and a green salad.

Coconut Curry with Chilli Rice

Preparation Time: 15 mins
Cooking Time: 25 mins
Serves: 4

300g Quorn Steak Strips
3 tbsp vegetable oil
1 onion, chopped
2 cloves of garlic, crushed
2 tbsp Thai red curry paste
400ml coconut milk
175g cherry tomatoes, halved
1 tbsp toasted desiccated coconut
2 tbsp fresh coriander plus extra for garnish.

For the chilli rice:-
300g Jasmine rice
1 red chilli, de-seeded and finely chopped
3 spring onions, trimmed and sliced
50g frozen peas

1. In a large frying pan, heat 2 tbsp of the oil, add the onion and garlic and cook for 3-4 minutes until softened. Stir in the curry paste and cook for 1 minute.

2. Stir in the Quorn Steak Strips and stir-fry for 5 minutes. Add the coconut milk and bring to the boil and simmer for 5 minutes.

3. While the steak strips are simmering, cook the rice according to pack instructions.

4. Heat the remaining 1 tbsp oil in a large frying pan or wok, add the chilli, spring onions and peas and stir-fry for 5 minutes, stir in the rice.

5. Toss the cherry tomatoes, desiccated coconut and chopped coriander into the curry and heat through for 2-3 minutes.

Serve the curry with the chilli rice and garnish with coriander.

Mushroom Stroganoff

A lovely winter warmer or quick midweek recipe served with rice or mashed potato.

Preparation Time: 10 mins
Cooking Time: 20 mins
Serves: 4

300g of Quorn Chicken Style Pieces or Quorn Steak Strips
2 tbsp vegetable oil
1 large red onion, thinly sliced
2 cloves garlic, crushed
225g brown cap or chestnut mushrooms, roughly chopped
2 tsp paprika
1 tbsp brandy (optional)
250ml vegetable stock
100g half fat crème fraîche
Chopped parsley and a sprinkle of paprika to garnish

1. Heat the oil in a non-stick frying pan and fry the onion and the garlic over a medium heat for 5 minutes. Add the Quorn Pieces or Strips, mushrooms and paprika and cook for a further 5 minutes.

2. Then add the brandy, stock and continue simmering gently for 5 minutes until the liquid is reduced by half.

3. Stir in the crème fraîche, season to taste and gently simmer for 3 minutes.

Garnish with chopped parsley and a sprinkle of paprika.

Moroccan Quorn Tagine

Preparation Time: 10 mins
Cooking Time: 45 mins
Serves: 4

350g Quorn Chicken Style Pieces

2 tbsp olive oil

1 large red onion, thinly sliced

2 garlic cloves, crushed

1½ tsp ground cumin

½ to 1 tbsp rose harissa paste

75g dried apricots, roughly chopped

400g tin chopped tomatoes

400ml boiling vegetable stock

400g tin chickpeas, drained

125g cherry tomatoes, halved

Small bunch coriander, chopped

250g couscous

1 tbsp olive oil

Small pinch salt

300ml boiling water

1. Heat the oil in a large saucepan and fry the onion for 5 minutes to soften. Stir in the Quorn Pieces, garlic, cumin and harissa paste. Cook for 2 minutes, stirring continuously.

2. Add the apricots, chopped tomatoes, stock and bring to the boil. Cover, reduce the heat and cook for 35 minutes to reduce and thicken the sauce.

3. Add the chickpeas and cherry tomatoes. Heat through.

4. Stir in half of the coriander and season to taste.

5. Put the couscous grains in a bowl and stir in the olive oil and salt to coat the grains. Pour on the boiling water and stir well. Cover with cling film and leave to stand for 5 minutes. Separate the grains with a fork just before serving with the tagine.

6. Garnish the tagine with the remaining chopped coriander and serve with the couscous.

Quorn Risotto

Delicious served with steamed green vegetables.

Preparation Time: 10 mins
Cooking Time: 25 mins
Serves: 4

300g Quorn Pieces
1 tbsp vegetable oil
1 medium onion, chopped
1 garlic clove, crushed
200g Arborio risotto rice
125ml white wine
550ml vegetable stock
25g butter
175g frozen peas
225g fresh young asparagus tips
50g fresh green pesto
100g fresh vegetarian cheese, grated
A handful of fresh basil leaves

1. Pre-heat 1 tbsp of oil in a large saucepan and cook the onions for 5 minutes until softened but not browned, add the garlic after 4 minutes.

2. Add the rice to the pan and stir well to coat with oil and become translucent, add the wine and simmer until it is all absorbed. Gradually add the stock a little at a time until it is nearly all absorbed, approximately 15-20 minutes. Stir occasionally.

3. Meanwhile in another frying pan melt the butter and fry the Quorn Pieces, peas and asparagus. Cook for 5 minutes until the pieces are golden. Add the Quorn Pieces, peas and asparagus to the rice and cook for a further 5-10 minutes, stirring occasionally, until the rice is cooked.

4. Stir in the pesto and half the grated vegetarian cheese.

5. Season to taste. Serve immediately sprinkled with the remaining cheese and roughly chopped basil leaves.

A Taste of
Takeaway

Moreish dishes that can be as
tasty as your favourite takeaway
and just as easy to deliver.

Quorn
Korma

Preparation Time: 10 mins
Cooking Time: 30 mins
Serves: 4

350g Quorn Chicken Style Pieces

2 shallots, peeled and halved

3 cloves garlic, peeled

1cm piece ginger, peeled

1 tbsp tomato purée

1½ tsp turmeric

1 tsp ground coriander

1 tsp ground cumin

½ tsp chilli powder

2 green cardamom pods, grains only

½ tsp ground cinnamon

100ml water

150ml coconut milk

1 tsp sugar

1 tbsp vegetable oil

1 tbsp desiccated coconut

1 tbsp butter

200ml single cream

Handful of chopped coriander

1. For the curry paste, purée the shallots, garlic, ginger, tomato purée, spices and water in a liquidiser or blender. Add the coconut milk and sugar and blend until smooth.

2. Heat the oil in a frying pan until hot, stir in the curry paste and Quorn Pieces, bring to the boil, stirring continuously for 3-4 minutes. Reduce the heat, cover and simmer for 20 minutes, stirring occasionally.

3. Add the desiccated coconut, butter and cream. Heat through and simmer over a low heat, stirring occasionally for 5 minutes. Season to taste and garnish with the chopped coriander.

Serve with Basmati rice and almonds.

Pad Thai
Noodles

Preparation Time: 10 mins
Cooking Time: 12 mins
Serves: 4

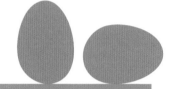

300g Quorn Chicken Style Pieces
260g pack of rice noodles
3 tbsp vegetable oil
1 red onion, thinly sliced into half moon shapes
3 garlic cloves, finely chopped
2-3 red chillies, de-seeded and finely chopped
4 tbsp light soy sauce
1 lime (juice only)
2 large free-range eggs, beaten

Garnish:
4 tbsp fresh coriander, roughly chopped
4 spring onions, chopped including the green part
75g dry roasted peanuts, roughly chopped

1. Cook the rice noodles following the pack instructions, refresh under cold running water and drain well, toss in 1 tbsp of the oil.

2. Heat the remaining oil in a wok over a high heat and stir-fry the Quorn Pieces for 3-4 minutes, add the red onion cook for a further 3 minutes. Add the garlic and chilli and stir-fry for 1-2 minutes more.

3. Pour in the soy sauce and lime juice, stir well, add in the noodles and toss for 1-2 minutes.

4. Pour over the beaten eggs slowly and evenly and let them begin to set (about 1 minute). Stir briefly until egg is cooked. Add half the garnish and stir through.

5. Serve with the remaining garnish scattered over the top.

Cook's Tip: Prepare all the ingredients first as this recipe is very quick once cooking starts.

Quorn Egg Fried Rice

Preparation Time: 15 mins
Cooking Time: 20 mins
Serves: 4

1 packet Quorn Fillets, defrosted* and sliced into 6 diagonally

1 tbsp rice wine vinegar

4cm piece root ginger, peeled and grated

2 tbsp vegetable oil

2 free-range eggs, beaten

2 garlic cloves, finely chopped

1 bunch spring onions, cut into fine rounds

1 red pepper, thinly sliced

½ yellow pepper, thinly sliced

½ green pepper, thinly sliced

300g Thai Jasmine rice (raw weight), boiled according to pack instructions

1 tbsp coriander, chopped

3 tbsp light soy sauce

1. Mix together the rice wine vinegar and half of the grated ginger then pour over the Quorn Fillets.

2. Heat a wok then add 1 tbsp of the vegetable oil, heat, add the eggs and cook as if you were making an omelette until set but not coloured. Put aside until cool and then cut into small pieces.

3. Heat up the rest of the oil in a wok and add the Quorn Fillet slices. Fry for 4 minutes or until golden, add the garlic, remaining ginger, spring onions and peppers and fry, tossing continuously for 2 minutes.

4. Add the cooked Thai rice and coriander, mixing with the Quorn Fillets and stir-fried vegetables. When hot, toss in the egg omelette and the light soy sauce and serve immediately.

* for defrost instructions refer to page 166

Singapore
Noodles

Preparation Time: 10 mins
Cooking Time: 10 mins
Serves: 4

350g Quorn Mince
6 tbsp hoisin sauce
1 clove fresh garlic, crushed
2 tbsp rice wine or dry sherry
1 red chilli, de-seeded and finely chopped, use
more or less depending on heat preference
2 tbsp light soy sauce
2 tbsp vegetable oil
100g mange tout, halved lengthways
6 spring onions, trimmed and chopped
180g dried medium egg noodles (3 blocks)
125g bean sprouts
200g pak choi, chopped

1. Combine the Quorn Mince, hoisin sauce, garlic, rice wine, chilli
   and soy sauce, mixing well. Heat half of the oil in a wok or stir-fry
   pan, then add the mince mixture and stir-fry over a high heat for
   2-3 minutes. Add the mange tout and half of the spring onions and
   stir-fry for a further 2 minutes.

2. Meanwhile cook the noodles according to the pack instructions.
   Drain and toss with the remaining vegetable oil.

3. Just before serving, stir the beansprouts and pak choi into the mince,
   allowing the pak choi to wilt slightly. Fork in the noodles and serve
   immediately, garnished with remaining spring onions.

Spicy Mexican Pizza

A spicy, tasty pizza full of Mexican flavour. As an alternative to the Quorn Fajita Strips, you could use Quorn Pieces and dust with your own Fajita seasoning.

Preparation Time: 10 mins
Cooking Time: 15-20 mins
Serves: 4

1 pack of Quorn Fajita Strips or 175g Quorn Chicken Style Pieces

200g tin chopped tomatoes

2 tbsp tomato purée

1 clove of garlic, crushed

1 level tsp crushed chilli flakes or to taste

2 heaped tbsp coriander, finely chopped

2 x 150g pizza bases

1 small red onion, thinly sliced

½ green pepper, thinly sliced

50g sweetcorn

100g Monteray Jack cheese or Cheddar, grated

1. Pre-heat the oven to 200°C (400°F/Gas Mark 6).

2. Mix together the chopped tomatoes, tomato purée, garlic, crushed chilli flakes and chopped coriander.

3. Place the 2 pizza bases on a baking tray and spread the tomato mixture evenly over them.

4. Scatter the Quorn Fajita Strips, red onion slices, green pepper and sweetcorn evenly over both of the pizzas and top with the grated cheese. Cook for 15-20 minutes until golden brown.

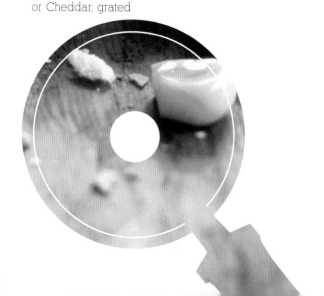

Stir-Fry Pieces in Black Bean Sauce

Preparation Time: 10 mins
Cooking Time: 10 mins
Serves: 4

300g Quorn Pieces or Quorn Steak Strips
250g broccoli, split into small florets
1 tbsp vegetable oil
1 small red onion, cut in half and sliced
2 garlic cloves, finely diced
2cm fresh ginger, grated
1 red pepper, de-seeded and sliced
1 425g jar black bean stir-fry sauce

1. Blanch the broccoli florets in boiling water for 1 minute, drain in a colander and refresh by pouring over cold water.

2. Heat a wok, add the oil and stir fry the Quorn Pieces, turning regularly for 4 minutes, add the onion, garlic and ginger and continue cooking for a further minute.

3. Add the pepper and stir-fry for 2 minutes until slightly softened, then add the broccoli florets and the black bean sauce.

4. Cook on high for a further 2-3 minutes until piping hot and then serve with egg noodles or rice.

Thai
Green Curry

Fresh Thai coconut based curry with Quorn Pieces, green vegetables, red peppers, baby corn and pak choi.

Preparation Time: 10 mins + 10 mins marinating
Cooking Time: 10 mins
Serves: 4

300g pack Quorn Chicken Style Pieces, defrosted*

2 tbsp light soy sauce

1-2 tbsp vegetable oil

2 tbsp green Thai curry paste

2 shallots, finely chopped

1 green chilli, de-seeded and finely chopped

3 garlic cloves, crushed

400g tin coconut milk

125g baby corn, blanched

125g green beans, trimmed and blanched

1 bunch fresh asparagus, trimmed and blanched

½ courgette cut into thin slices

1 red pepper, de-seeded and cut into thin strips

125g pak choi leaves, separated and washed

1 tbsp lime juice

Small bunch of fresh coriander, chopped

2 spring onions, trimmed & thinly shredded

1. Marinate the Quorn Pieces in the light soy sauce for up to 10 minutes.

2. Heat the oil in a wok, add the green Thai curry paste and cook for 2 minutes stirring frequently.

3. Add the shallots, chilli and garlic and stir-fry for 2 minutes. Stir in the marinated Quorn Pieces and fry for 1 minute.

4. Pour in the coconut milk and bring to a simmering point. Add the blanched baby corn, green beans, asparagus, courgettes and red pepper. Cook over a medium heat for 3-4 minutes, stirring continuously. Add the pak choi and cover with a lid for 1 minute to steam and wilt the leaves. Stir in the fresh lime juice and half the chopped coriander.

5. Serve sprinkled with the remaining coriander and the spring onions.

Accompany with Thai Jasmine rice.

* for defrost instructions refer to page 166

150

Sour -Fry

Prepa... ...e: 15 mins + 20 mins marinating
Cooking ... . 15 mins
Serves: 4

350g Quorn Chicken Style Pieces

6 tbsp fresh orange juice

2 tbsp dry sherry

1 tbsp dark soy sauce

4 tbsp rice wine vinegar

2 garlic cloves, finely chopped

2 tbsp sesame or vegetable oil

1 bunch spring onions, finely chopped

400g stir-fry mixed vegetables of your choice e.g. sliced yellow and red pepper, mange tout, baby corn, sliced courgettes, bamboo shoots etc.

100ml vegetable stock

1 tbsp clear honey

1½ level tsp cornflour

1. Place the Quorn Pieces in a bowl. Mix together the orange juice, sherry, soy sauce, wine vinegar and garlic, pour over the Quorn Pieces. Cover and marinate for 20 minutes.

2. Remove Quorn Pieces reserving the marinade. Heat half of the oil in a wok or large frying pan, add the Quorn Pieces and stir-fry for 5 minutes.

3. Add the remaining oil and fry the spring onions and all the mixed vegetables for 4-5 minutes or until just tender, but still crunchy.

4. Mix the reserved marinade with the vegetable stock, honey and cornflour and stir into the vegetables. Cover and simmer for 2-3 minutes, season to taste. Serve at once with noodles or rice.

Quorn
Tikka Masala

Preparation Time: 5 mins + 30 mins marinating
Cooking Time: 45 mins
Serves: 4

300g Quorn Chicken
Style Pieces

For the Marinade:
2 tbsp good quality
Tikka Masala paste
1 tbsp ground cumin
1 tbsp ground coriander
½ tbsp turmeric
1 tsp chilli powder
140ml Greek style thick
set yogurt
1 tbsp tomato purée
2 cloves garlic, finely
chopped

For the curry:
1 tbsp vegetable oil
2 medium onions,
finely chopped
1 large red pepper,
de-seeded and diced
400ml hot vegetable stock
2 tbsp coriander leaves,
freshly chopped

1. Mix all the marinade ingredients together in a bowl. Add the Quorn Pieces and stir until evenly coated. Leave to marinate for at least 30 minutes.

2. Heat the oil in a saucepan and fry the onions over a medium heat for 5 minutes until soft and golden, add the pepper and fry for a couple of minutes.

3. Add the Quorn Pieces and the marinade to the pan and stir-fry for 10 minutes, to cook out the spices. Gradually add the hot stock, mixing well, and bring to the boil. Reduce the heat, cover and simmer for at least 30 minutes to allow the spices to blend together and mellow. Top up with a little boiling water if necessary.

Serve with a sprinkling of freshly chopped coriander and boiled rice.

Little
Chefs

Easy, yummy recipes
for kids to do, that
will definitely leave
clean plates too.

WARNING:
May cause messy
kitchens!

Sweet Potato Curry

A fantastic recipe for children to both prepare and enjoy. For a spicier version just add more of the red Thai paste.

Preparation Time: 5 mins
Cooking Time: 25 mins
Serves: 4

350g Quorn Chicken Style Pieces
½ tbsp red Thai curry paste
300g sweet potato, peeled and cut into 2½cm cubes
400ml coconut milk
1 vegetable stock cube
3 tbsp fresh coriander, chopped

1. Pre-heat a wok and stir-fry the curry paste for 1-2 minutes, stirring continuously to prevent burning. Add the Quorn Pieces and sweet potato and fry, stirring continuously.

2. Add the coconut milk, crumble in the vegetable stock cube, increase heat but do not boil. Reduce heat and simmer uncovered for 20 minutes or until the sweet potatoes are cooked.

3. Scatter over the chopped coriander and serve with boiled rice and steamed green vegetables.

Quorn Fillets work well in this too, either whole or sliced.

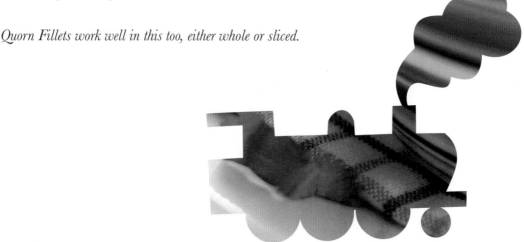

Cheese & Onion Burgers

This is a really easy recipe that kids would enjoy making and eating...

Preparation Time: 10 mins
Cooking Time: 15 mins
Serves: 4

175g Quorn Mince defrost* if using frozen

1 tbsp vegetable oil

1 small red onion, finely diced

1 tsp dried rosemary

2 slices of wholemeal bread, made into crumbs

40g mature Cheddar cheese, grated

75g low fat cream cheese

1 tbsp yeast extract dissolved in 1 tbsp boiling water

1 tbsp fresh parsley, finely chopped

1 medium free-range egg, beaten

Extra oil for frying the burgers

1. Pre-heat the oil in a frying pan over a medium heat, add the red onion and dried rosemary and cook gently for 5 minutes, until the onion is softened but not browned.

2. In a large mixing bowl combine the Quorn Mince and breadcrumbs with the cooked onion and rosemary. Add in the grated cheese and cream cheese, mixing well to distribute the cream cheese throughout the mix.

3. Stir through the yeast extract and parsley, then add the beaten egg, seasoning and mix well.

4. Take a handful of mix and firmly compress into a burger shape approx 2 cm in thickness. Makes approx. 8 burgers.

5. To cook the burgers, pre-heat a little oil in a large non-stick frying pan over a medium heat. Add the burgers allowing sufficient space between them for turning. Cook for 4 minutes, then turn over and continue cooking for another 4 minutes or until the burgers are piping hot.

Delicious served in a burger bun or pitta bread with crispy lettuce leaves and jacket potato wedges.

* for defrost instructions refer to page 166

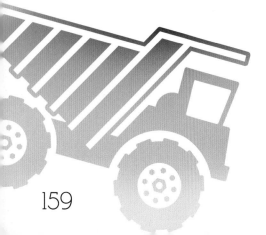

Sausage & Crushed Potato Pie

A basic pie with a simple twist, guaranteed to impress all the family…

Preparation Time: 10 mins
Cooking Time: 35 mins
Serves: 4

1 pack Quorn Sausages
2 tbsp vegetable oil
1 onion, finely chopped
1 420g can baked beans
4 tbsp tomato ketchup
1 tbsp brown sauce
80ml water

Topping Ingredients:
750g potatoes, peeled and cut into chunks
1 tbsp olive oil
75g Cheddar cheese, grated
1 tbsp fresh parsley, chopped (optional)

1. Pre-heat oven to 200°C (400°F/Gas Mark 6).

2. Boil potatoes until just cooked, drain and crush or mash then add the oil, cheese, parsley and season to taste.

3. Meanwhile in a large frying pan pre-heat 1 tbsp of oil and brown the Quorn Sausages turning frequently. This should take 2-3 minutes or until golden, then remove sausages from the pan and set to one side. Add the remaining oil to the pan and soften the onion for about 5 minutes.

4. Cut each sausage diagonally into 4 pieces and return to the pan along with the baked beans, ketchup, brown sauce and water. Bring up to a simmer and continue cooking gently for 5 minutes.

5. Place the mixture into an ovenproof dish, top with the crushed potato topping and bake for 15 minutes until the top is golden.

Serve with seasonal vegetables.

Index

Cookery Notes

- All spoon measurements are level, unless specified otherwise.

- Ovens & grills should be pre-heated to the specified temperature.

- Where seasoning is mentioned this refers to salt and freshly ground black pepper, added to taste.

- All recipes are tested using semi-skimmed milk, unless specified otherwise.

- Once cooked, Quorn recipe dishes can be stored in the fridge for up to 24 hours or placed in the freezer for up to 1 month (assuming all other ingredients are also suitable for freezing and re-heating).

- Ensure recipe dishes are cold before placing in the fridge or freezer.

- Please defrost thoroughly before re-heating, and ensure all food is piping hot before serving.

Liquid

Imperial	Metric
¼ pint	150 ml
½ pint	300 ml
1 pint	600 ml
1 ½ pint	900 ml
1 ¾ pint	1 litre

Weights

Metric	Imperial
1 oz	25 g
2 oz	50 g
4 oz	125 g
8 oz	225 g
12 oz	350 g
14 oz	400 g
16 oz (1lb)	450 g

All oven cooking times are using fan assisted ovens.

All these are approximate conversions, which have either been rounded up or down. Never mix metric and imperial measures in one recipe; stick to one system or the other.

Defrosting
Instructions

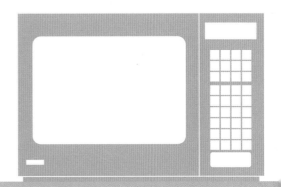

Most Quorn products cook well from frozen, however if the recipe calls for skewering or has a marinade, here at the Quorn Kitchen, we recommend you defrost the products first.

Quorn products are easier to skewer once defrosted and if using a marinade, the flavours are better absorbed by defrosted products.

Ideally, you should always defrost your Quorn products overnight in the fridge. However, if you're feeling a little more spontaneous, Quorn products also defrost well in the microwave:

*Defrost using an 800w microwave on the **defrost setting**:*

1. Place Quorn products in a microwaveable bowl, cover with microwavable film and pierce several times.

2. Using the **defrost setting** on the microwave, set the relevant products to the relevant timings:

Quorn Pieces
For 300g, on **defrost power** for 8-10 minutes, shaking halfway.

Quorn Fillets
For 6 fillets, on **defrost power** for 8-10 minutes, shaking half way.

Quorn Sausages
For 6 Sausages, on **defrost power** for 8-10 minutes, shaking half way.

These times are for guidelines only as each microwave varies.

Notes